GRAPHIC LIBRARY™

INVENTIONS AND DISCOVERY

THOMAS EDISON and the LIGHTBULB

by Scott R. Welvaert

illustrated by Phil Miller and
Charles Barnett III

Consultant:
Hal Wallace
Historian, Electricity Collections
National Museum of American History
Smithsonian Institution, Washington, D.C.

Capstone

Mankato, Minnesota

Graphic Library is published by Capstone Press,
151 Good Counsel Drive, P.O. Box 669, Mankato, Minnesota 56002.
www.capstonepress.com

1 2 3 4 5 6 11 10 09 08 07 06

Library of Congress Cataloging-in-Publication Data
Welvaert, Scott R.
Thomas Edison and the lightbulb / by Scott Welvaert; illustrated by Phil Miller and
Charles Barnett III.
p. cm.—(Graphic library. Inventions and discovery)
Summary: "In graphic novel format, tells the story of Thomas Edison's involvement in the
development of the incandescent lightbulb"—Provided by publisher.
Includes bibliographical references and index.
ISBN-13: 978-0-7368-6489-3 (hardcover)
ISBN-10: 0-7368-6489-X (hardcover)
ISBN-13: 978-0-7368-7524-0 (softcover pbk.)
ISBN-10: 0-7368-7524-7 (softcover pbk.)
1. Edison, Thomas A. (Thomas Alva), 1847–1931—Juvenile literature. 2. Inventors—United
States—Biography—Juvenile literature. 3. Electric engineering—United States—History—
Juvenile literature. I. Title. II. Series.
TK140.E3P37 2007
621.3092—dc22
                                                                  2006006976

Art Direction and Design
Bob Lentz

Colorist
Buzz Setzer

Editor
Christopher Harbo

TABLE OF CONTENTS

This gauge measures pressure changes on the button.

I can calculate the heat from the corona based on the gauge's readings.

Amazing!

With another success under his belt, Edison relaxed with his fellow scientists.

You know, Thomas, I've heard some scientists are close to perfecting an electric lamp. Just imagine a city lit up like these stars light up the sky.

It would be beautiful. But building a lamp is only half the problem. You would need a reliable supply of electrical power as well.

In September 1878, Edison and his assistant Charles Batchelor visited William Wallace's shop in Ansonia, Connecticut. Wallace was working on a machine called a dynamo that generated electricity.

The magnet spins, creating an electric current.

Could dozens of dynamos be connected to form a citywide electric network, William?

It's possible. But you'd need more insulated wire than I can imagine.

Can we improve on this dynamo technology?

I don't see why not.

Then we'll use the dynamo as our power source. Now all we need is a long-lasting lightbulb.

CHAPTER 3
BUILDING A BETTER LIGHTBULB

In October 1878, Francis R. Upton, an engineer, joined Edison's team. He studied the work other scientists had done on incandescent lighting.

I looked into all the patents. Most scientists have had trouble getting enough air out of their bulbs.

Right. Without enough vacuum, their filaments burn up too quickly.

What do you want to do?

Perhaps we can avoid the vacuum issue altogether by using platinum filaments. Platinum doesn't need vacuum to glow.

What are you suggesting, Lowrey?

We need to take legal action against Swan United. They are infringing upon our patents.

Edison and his lawyers knew it may not be an easy victory. They needed another plan.

While you worked with platinum, Swan built a carbon lamp. His didn't work as well as yours, but we need to tread lightly.

Then I suggest we press for a merger of the two companies.

Meanwhile . . .

You failed to apply for patents, Joseph. Edison has the legal edge.

What should we do?

We should make a deal. Edison has offered a merger.

The agreement formed the Ediswan Company in London, England. Swan made money on his ideas and Edison was allowed to continue his work on his lightbulb.

After his success in Paris, Edison set his sights on lighting a square mile area near Pearl and Fulton Streets in New York City. In 1882, he personally installed the lighting system at Drexel, Morgan & Company.

How did you figure out a way to do all of this?

Hard work, my friend. There is no substitute for hard work.

Later that year, Pearl Street Station began making electricity for customers.

Edison's lightbulbs and electrical power system started off small. In its first few years, Pearl Street Station served about 500 customers.

But demand for electrical light and power grew . . .

. . . until electric light graced all of New York City.

With his inventions, Edison and the inventors who followed him changed the world.

The dangers of gas and oil lighting were replaced with the soft glow of incandescent lighting.

Travel by night became easier and much safer.

Electric light showed us a whole new side to our streets and towns.

MORE ABOUT THOMAS EDISON and the LIGHTBULB

- Thomas Alva Edison was born February 11, 1847, in Milan, Ohio. He died on October 18, 1931, in West Orange, New Jersey.

- Edison opened his laboratory in Menlo Park, New Jersey, in 1876. His laboratory became known as the "invention factory" because Edison's staff often worked on more than one invention at a time. Because of his amazing inventions, newspapers called Edison the "Wizard of Menlo Park."

- Edison patented 1,093 inventions in his lifetime. Besides the lightbulb, he developed the phonograph for recording and playing sounds. He also invented the movie camera and made some of the world's first silent movies.

- Edison's first lightbulbs burned for less than 100 hours. Eventually, he produced a lightbulb that burned for more than 1,500 hours.

- The lightbulb was only one part of Edison's effort to bring electric light to the world. He also developed circuit breakers, transmission lines, fuses, light sockets, and light switches to make electric light safe and easy to use.

Edison developed a dynamo he called Jumbo to create electricity in his Pearl Street Station. The Jumbo dynamo was four times as large as any dynamo built at the time. It produced enough electricity to power 1,200 lights. Pearl Street Station used six Jumbo dynamos to supply power to 1 square mile (2.6 square kilometers) of New York City.

Near his laboratory, Edison had factories that made some of his inventions. In 1882, Edison's factories made about 100,000 lightbulbs. But demand for electric light grew quickly. In 1900, his factories made 45 million lightbulbs.

When Pearl Street Station opened in 1882, it served 85 customers with about 400 lightbulbs. Fourteen months later, the power station served 508 customers with more than 12,700 lightbulbs.

GLOSSARY

carbon (KAR-buhn)—an element found in diamonds, coal, and living plants and animals; carbon filaments were made by baking materials until they turned into pure carbon.

corona (kuh-ROH-nuh)—the outermost part of the sun's atmosphere

dynamo (DYE-nuh-moh)—a machine for converting the power of a turning wheel into electricity

filament (FIL-uh-muhnt)—a thin wire that is heated electrically to produce light

incandescent (in-kan-DESS-uhnt)—glowing with strong light and heat

patent (PAT-ent)—a document that protects people's inventions so others cannot steal the ideas

vacuum (VAK-yoom)—a sealed space emptied of air or gas

INTERNET SITES

FactHound offers a safe, fun way to find Internet sites related to this book. All of the sites on FactHound have been researched by our staff.

Here's how:
1. Visit *www.facthound.com*
2. Choose your grade level.
3. Type in this book ID **073686489X** for age-appropriate sites. You may also browse subjects by clicking on letters, or by clicking on pictures and words.
4. Click on the **Fetch It** button.

FactHound will fetch the best sites for you!

READ MORE

Cefrey, Holly. *The Inventions of Thomas Alva Edison: Father of the Light Bulb and the Motion Picture Camera.* Reading Power. New York: PowerKids Press, 2003.

Nobleman, Marc Tyler. *The Light Bulb.* Great Inventions. Mankato, Minn.: Capstone Press, 2004.

Price-Groff, Claire. *Thomas Alva Edison: Inventor and Entrepreneur.* Great Life Stories. New York: Franklin Watts, 2003.

Raatma, Lucia. *Thomas Edison.* Early Biographies. Minneapolis: Compass Point Books, 2004.

BIBLIOGRAPHY

Baldwin, Neil. *Edison: Inventing the Century.* Chicago: University of Chicago Press, 2001.

Friedel, Robert, and Paul Israel. *Edison's Electric Light: Biography of an Invention.* New Brunswick, N.J.: Rutgers University Press, 1986.

Josephson, Matthew. *Edison: A Biography.* New York: McGraw-Hill, 1959.

Millard, A. J. *Edison and the Business of Innovation.* Baltimore: Johns Hopkins University Press, 1990.

INDEX